psalms
of
forgiveness

D1716155

Timothy Brown, S.J.

ISBN: 978-1-62720-143-8

Published by Apprentice House

Apprentice House
Communication Department
Loyola University Maryland
4501 N. Charles Street
Baltimore, MD 21210
410.617.5265 • 410.617.2198 (fax)
www.ApprenticeHouse.com
info@ApprenticeHouse.com

to Jack Dennis, S.J.

Cover

The art on the cover was painted by John Murray Dennis, MD

table of contents

"Fall down 53 times.

Get up 54."

— *Zen saying*

introduction

—Preface—

If you bring your gift to the altar and there recall that
your brother or sister has anything against you
Leave your gift
Leave it

Go first
Be reconciled
And then come back
Those are Jesus's words to you

Ask God for strength
The grace will follow

I heard a spiritual director say one time that
forgiving does not mean putting the other one on
probation
No
God's way is bilateral not unilateral
Two sided
Reconciliation is a two way street

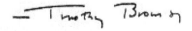

——The Inspiration——

During the course of my illness I turned to the Psalms. I used a wonderful volume, The Psalms with Commentary by Kathleen Norris. In the Introduction to her book, she writes:

> The God one encounters in the Psalms is God as human beings have experienced him as both awake and asleep, gloriously present and lamentably absent, and above all, various. A warrior who stands up for us, a mother who holds us to her breast. An eagle sheltering us under her wing, and a creator who brings forth lightning, wind, and rain from the storehouses of heaven. The Psalms work in the way that all great poetry works, allowing us to enter no matter who we are or what we believe, or don't believe; addressing us at the deepest, level — what Saint Benedict might term "the ear of the heart."

I also found myself drawn to the language of the King James version of the Psalms. Why the King James version, with its lack of inclusive language, you might wonder? Again, Kathleen Norris puts it so well:

> One reader of a Jesuit magazine wrote an angry letter to complain about an article that had prominently featured a quotation from John Donne: "No man is an island." The editors commented that since Mr. Donne had died in

1631 they had no means of inviting him to revise his grammar for the more "inclusive" modern era. To read and appreciate seventeenth-century verse, or the King James Bible, one must favor imagination over ideology, and discover for oneself the inclusivity that is there. But this is an increasingly difficult task in our literal-minded age.

But many poets who write in English regard the King James as the literary standard by which to judge subsequent translations of the Bible. The story of this translation — so called because it was commissioned by King James I of England early in the seventeenth century — is a story about the power and primacy of vivid language and pleasurable speech, words that hold the attention of the ear and provide physical images pleasing to the mind's eye. The translation has so embedded itself into the English language that most people are unaware that many images and phrases still in use entered the idiom through the King James: 'my cup runneth over', 'all flesh is grass', 'on eagles' wings', 'tender mercies; 'loaves and fishes; 'lilies of the field; 'salt of the earth', 'through a glass, darkly', 'where your treasure is, there will your heart be also'.

So I ask you to join me in praying through the Psalms — in imagery that is poetic but not inclusive in the literal sense of the meaning. The images evoked should be vivid and will provide a great deal of comfort. Join me in your prayer.

acts of mercy

— Psalm 89 —

I will sing of the mercies of the Lord forever; With
my mouth will I make known Your faithfulness
to all generations.

For I have said, "Mercy shall be built up forever; Your
faithfulness You shall establish in the very
heavens."

"I have made a covenant with My chosen, I have
sworn to My servant David:

'Your seed I will establish forever, And build up your
throne to all generations.'"

And the heavens will praise Your wonders, O Lord;
Your faithfulness also in the assembly of the
saints.

O Lord God of hosts, Who *is* mighty like You, O
Lord? Your faithfulness also surrounds You.

You rule the raging of the sea; When its waves rise,
You still them.

The heavens *are* Yours, the earth also *is* Yours; The world and all its fullness, You have founded them.

The north and the south, You have created them; Tabor and Hermon rejoice in Your name.

You have a mighty arm; Strong is Your hand, *and* high is Your right hand.

Righteousness and justice *are* the foundation of Your throne; Mercy and truth go before Your face.

———— // ————

Every soul is like a tiny drop
without which the whole world would thirst

To understand is to stand under

Which is to look up to

Which is a good way to understand

— Corita

— Works of Mercy —

The Corporal works of mercy:
- To feed the hungry;
- To give drink to the thirsty;
- To clothe the naked;
- To harbor the harborless;
- To visit the sick;
- To ransom the captive;
- To bury the dead

The spiritual works of mercy:
- To instruct the ignorant;
- To counsel the doubtful;
- To admonish sinners;
- To bear wrongs patiently;
- To forgive offenses willingly;
- To comfort the afflicted
- To pray for the living and the dead

—— // ——

— Proverbs 12:18 —

Thoughtless words can pierce like a sword,

but the tongue of the wise brings healing.

That's why we're here tonight. We have all chosen to come here—all of us—to acknowledge our ordinary human misery. It is a fact of life, part of being alive. The worst of us and the best of us are here to admit it.

The occasional coldness, the compulsions, the need, the pains, the frustrations, the impatience, the failure to reach out, the paralyzing fears, the meanness we don't really mean.

The grudges we nurse, the wounds we keep unhealed, the self pity, the self-pride, the expectations never quite met, the love only sometimes returned, the thirst no water—no wine—can quench.

It is remarkable that we Christians can come here together for this. It is remarkable that we show our faces to each other, sit next to each other with the lights on… and say to each other by our presence here and say to another sinful human being in the sacramental encounter I AM A SINNER AND I HAVE SINNED.

We human, beings—all of us—are sinners and our ordinary human misery loves company.

MORE THAN THAT, MISERY NEEDS COMPANY.

And that is probably what gets us into trouble in the first place. That is probably at the root of so much of our sin, our ordinary human misery. Aware of our needs, we search for that which will fulfill those needs.

Most often our basic goodness triumphs. We find and give ourselves over to that love, that friendship, that form of service that gives real meaning to life.

But sometimes we look for the answer in all the wrong places.

We proceed to look feverishly for what will keep us eternally warm, secure and comfortable. And that which only God can give we are tempted to look for in a car, or in clothes or in cosmetic surgery, or in our children's accomplishments.

We look sometimes for love, understanding and security in all the wrong places. We worship idols of chrome and ego instead of God.

Or else we play God—we don't do a very good job of it either. We decide not to forgive those who hurt us. And we find ourselves far too often unable to forgive ourselves.

The point in both these miserable human tendencies— worshiping idols and playing God—is that we don't let God be God. We don't always really want to come to God. We don't really want God to touch us. We don't always really want the pleasure of God's company.

But like it or not, misery HAS company.

Nothing can separate us from the love of God. We should rejoice that God has brought us this far. We should rejoice that He wants our company—even in our sinfulness, our imperfection, our feeble attempts to find love and truth in things that fade and fail.

What is important about our coming here tonite is not that we remember every sinful moment of the past weeks, months or even years...

BUT

That we present our ordinary human misery alongside our ordinary human goodness—to God.

What is important is not so much that we do penance for our sins, but that we allow ourselves to be refreshed by the healing hand of God.

What is important is not that we forever successfully lock Satan out of our lives but that we really for just five minutes let God IN.

— John Ciani, S.J.

Late have I loved you, O beauty ever ancient, ever
new!

Late have I loved you

and behold, you were within, and I without and
without
I sought you.

And deformed, I ran after those forms of beauty
you have made.

You were with me, and I was not with you, those
things
held me back from you, things whose only
being was to be in you.

You called; you cried; and you broke through my
deafness.

You flashed; you shone; and you chased away my
blindness.

You became fragrant; and I inhaled and sighed for
you.

I tasted, and now hunger and thirst for you.

You touched me, and I burned for your embrace.

— *St. Augustine*

—The Woman Taken in Adultery—

John 8:2–11

Early in the morning he came again to the temple. All the people came to him and he sat down and began to teach them. The scribes and the Pharisees brought a woman who had been caught in adultery; and making her stand before all of them, they said to him, "Teacher, this woman was caught in the very act of committing adultery. Now in the law Moses commanded us to stone such women. Now what do you say?" They said this to test him, so that they might have some charge to bring against him. Jesus bent down and wrote with his finger on the ground.

When they kept on questioning him, he straightened up and said to them, "Let anyone among you who is without sin be the first to throw a stone at her." And once again he bent down and wrote on the ground. When they heard it, they went away, one by one, beginning with the elders; and Jesus was left alone with the woman standing before him. Jesus straightened up and said to her, "Woman, where are they? Has no one condemned you?"

She said, "No one, sir."

And Jesus said, "Neither do I condemn you. Go your way, and from now on do not sin again."

—— The Spirit of Forgiveness ——

Let me ask you this ......

Have you ever kept quiet even though you wanted to defend yourself when you felt you were treated unfairly by another member of the family?

That's the experience of the Holy Spirit—

Have you ever forgiven someone even though you got no thanks for it and that silent forgiveness of yours ended up being taken for granted? —the Holy Spirit—

Have you ever listened to your spouse or your mother or brother—not because you had to; nor because it would mean keeping the peace—but simply because you knew that was the right thing to do—the Holy Spirit—

And have you ever sacrificed something without receiving thanks or recognition for it—and felt alright with that? the Holy Spirit—

Again... Many more experiences... Somehow I feel sure that the most direct route to experiencing the Holy Spirit in our hearts and in our homes is to ask for the grace to give; to share, to console one another; to bandage a hurting wound, to lift a fallen human spirit, to mend a quarrel, to search out a forgotten friend, to dismiss a suspicion and replace it with trust, to encourage, to keep a promise, to bury an old grudge, to express gratitude, to tell someone you love them and then tell them again—to notice the Spirit of Christ already within —The Spirit of Christ—the spirit that manifests itself in the family here

— Anonymous

acceptance

I said, "Lord, be merciful to me; Heal my soul, for I
   have sinned against You."

My enemies speak evil of me: "When will he die, and
   his name perish?"

And if he comes to see *me*, he speaks lies; His heart
   gathers iniquity to itself; *When* he goes out, he
   tells *it*.

All who hate me whisper together against me;
   Against me they devise my hurt.

"An evil disease," *they say*, "clings to him. And *now*
   that he lies down, he will rise up no more."

Even my own familiar friend in whom I trusted, Who
   ate my bread, Has lifted up *his* heel against me.

But You, O Lord, be merciful to me, and raise me up,
   That I may repay them.

By this I know that You are well pleased with me,
   Because my enemy does not triumph over me.

As for me, You uphold me in my integrity, And set
   me before Your face forever.

Blessed *be* the Lord God of Israel From everlasting to
   everlasting! Amen and Amen.

— The Prodigal Son —

Luke 15:11–32

Then Jesus said, "There was a man who had two sons. The younger of them said to his father, 'Father, give me the share of the property that will belong to me.'" So he divided his property between them.

A few days later the younger son gathered all he had and traveled to a distant country, and there he squandered his property in dissolute living. When he had spent everything, a severe famine took place throughout that country, and he began to be in need. So he went and hired himself out to one of the citizens of that country, who sent him to his fields to feed the pigs. He would gladly have filled himself with the pods that the pigs were eating; and no one gave him anything.

But when he came to himself he said, 'How many of my father's hired hands have bread enough and to spare, but here I am dying of hunger! I will get up and go to my father, and I will say to him, "Father, I have sinned against heaven and before you; I am no longer worthy to be called your son; treat me like one of your hired hands."' So he set off and went to his father. But while he was still far off, his father saw him and was filled with compassion; he ran and put his arms around him and kissed him. Then the son said to him, 'Father, I have sinned against heaven and before you; I am no longer worthy to be called your son.' But the father said to his slaves, 'Quickly, bring out a robe—the best one—and put it on him; put a ring on his finger and sandals on his feet. And get the fatted calf and kill it, and let us eat and celebrate; for this son of mine was dead and is alive again; he was lost and is found!' And they began to celebrate.

"Now his elder son was in the field; and when he came and approached the house, he heard music and dancing. He called one of the slaves and asked what was going on. He replied, 'Your brother has come, and your father has killed the fatted calf, because he has got him back safe and sound.' Then he became angry and refused to go in. His father came out and began to plead with him. But he answered his father, 'Listen! For all these years I have been working like a slave for you, and I have never disobeyed your command; yet you have never given me even a young goat so that I might celebrate with my friends. But when this son of yours came back, who has devoured your property with prostitutes, you killed the fatted calf for him!' Then the father said to him, 'Son, you are always with me, and all that is mine is yours. But we had to celebrate and rejoice, because this brother of yours was dead and has come to life; he was lost and has been found.'"

— **Proverbs 4:25–27** —

Let your eyes be fixed ahead,
    your gaze be straight before you.
Let the path you tread be level
    and all your ways be firm.
Turn neither to right nor to left,
    keep your foot clear of evil.

— Jesus as the Prodigal Son —

Frere Pierre Marie, the founder of the Fraternity of Jerusalem, a community of monks living in the city, reflects on Jesus as the prodigal son in a very poetic and biblical way. He writes:

> He, who is born not from human stock, or human desire or human will, but from God himself, one day took to himself everything that was under his footstool and he left with his inheritance, his title of Son, and the whole ransom price. He left for a far country ... the faraway land ... where he became as human beings are and emptied himself. His own people did not accept him and his first bed was a bed of straw! Like a root in arid ground, he grew up before us, he was despised, the lowest of men, before whom one covers his face. Very soon, he came to know exile, hostility, loneliness ... After having given away everything in a life of bounty, his worth, his peace, his light, his truth, his life ... all the treasures of knowledge and wisdom and the hidden mystery kept secret for endless ages; after having lost himself among the lost children of the house of Israel, spending his time with the sick (and not with the well-to-do), with the sinners (and not with the just), and even with the prostitutes to whom he promised entrance into the Kingdom of his Father; after having been treated

as a glutton and a drunkard, as a friend of tax collectors and sinners, as a Samaritan, a possessed, a blasphemer; after having offered everything, even his body and his blood; after having felt deeply in himself sadness, anguish, and a troubled soul; after having gone to the bottom of despair, with which he voluntarily dressed himself as being abandoned by his Father far away from the source of living water, he cried out from the cross on which he was nailed: "I am thirsty." He was laid to rest in the dust and the shadow of death. And there, on the third day, he rose up from the depths of hell to where he had descended, burdened with the crimes of us all, he bore our sins, our sorrows he carried. Standing straight, he cried out: "Yes, I am ascending to my Father, and your Father, to my God, and your God." And he ascended to heaven. Then in the silence, looking at his Son and all his children, since his Son had become all in all, the Father said to his servants, "Quick! Bring out the best robe and put it on him; put a ring on his finger and sandals on his feet; let us eat and celebrate! Because my children who, as you know, were dead have returned to life; they were lost and have been found again! My prodigal Son has brought them all back." They all began to have a feast dressed in their long robes, washed white in the blood of the Lamb.

— Frere Pierre Marie

Lord Jesus, through the power of the Holy Spirit,

Go back into my memory as I sleep.

Every hurt that has ever been done to me, heal that hurt.

Every hurt that I have ever caused to another person, heal that hurt.

All the relationships that have been damaged in my whole life that I am not aware of, heal those relationships.

But, Lord, if there is anything that I need to do,

If I need to go to a person because he or she is still suffering from my hand,

Bring to my awareness that person.

I choose to forgive, and I ask to be forgiven.

Remove whatever bitterness may be in my heart, Lord,

And fill the empty spaces with your love. Amen.

— Francis X. Knott, S.J.

—— Perseverance ——

When Fr. Brown asked me to write about forgiveness, the first thoughts that came to mind were not about forgiveness, but about the two people in my life I have found it most difficult to forgive and with whom, hard as I try, I am not sure I will ever achieve the peace of total forgiveness. The one I will discuss here is my former husband.

But first, a bit of my background. I was the only child of two wonderful loving, solid, moral and upstanding parents. Both were born and bred in New England. My childhood and high school years were very happy ones. I met my future husband, nine years my senior, when he began coaching our parochial school eighth grade basketball team. Over the years a friendship, then a relationship developed. Ours was looked upon as a "fairy tale romance." We married when I was twenty, and he was twenty-nine. In the traditional Catholic way, we immediately had three sons in three and a half years.

We were both involved volunteering with the youth of our parish and in our children's activities. People looked upon us as the "ideal/perfect" young family.

Then the bottom fell out. Nine and a half years into the marriage, this man whom I adored, arrived home around 2:00 a.m. on a Friday night four days before Christmas. (I had been frantic, thinking he must have been in an accident.) Recalling the next eight words he said to me sting even to this day, over forty-five years later: "I might as well tell you, we're through." If a bomb had exploded in that room, it wouldn't have equaled the impact of the explosion in my heart and in my life.

As I collapsed in tears, he very calmly told me he had fallen in love with his secretary, was having an affair with her and wanted to leave me and our three sons. It sounded to me like, at age twenty-nine, my life was over. Somehow God gave me the strength, despite my devastation, to put on a front and get through the holidays. On January 11, he left, stepping over his crying children and ignoring them as he carried his clothes out to our car.

I had to 'face the music' immediately. Four teams he coached for the parish CYO had games the next day. I called people to handle the boys' teams, and I coached the girls. (Thank God they were good, because I was in no condition to do anything.) Coaching those girls turned out to be a true gift from the good Lord. I coached for nine years—until I needed the time to attend my sons' games—and several of these young women are still dear friends of mine today.

That fateful night, I made three decisions that I continue to honor: 1) I wouldn't marry again, if ever, until the boys were grown. I didn't want to put them through any unnecessary trauma; 2) I would never drink alone, which was kind of humorous because I rarely drink at all. I had seen too many women destroy their lives with alcohol; 3) I would try to be upbeat, not maudlin, around family and friends. Waking up each morning and facing another day of loneliness was the hardest for me. Reflecting on how I was going to make it with these three young children, little money and no job was overwhelming. I began each day reciting the Serenity Prayer:

> God, grant me the serenity to accept the things I cannot change, the courage to change the things I can and the wisdom to know the difference.

I even taped it to my bathroom mirror. It was my lifesaver.

Our marriage counselor said, "Why aren't you furious, throwing chairs, etc.?" I couldn't think about being mad. I just wanted him back, and I was willing to forgive him However, his return was not going to happen.

Soon the repercussions began to manifest themselves in our oldest son. At eight years old, I found him about to jump off a porch roof outside his bedroom and commit suicide. He underwent years of psychiatric care, but got into drugs at an early age and went from being the smartest student and best athlete in his class to dropping out of school at fifteen and becoming a heroin addict. At that time, things were totally out of hand with this very troubled boy. I consulted four different psychiatrists for advice. Each of them told me that, in order to save my other two sons, I had to remove my oldest from our home. This shattered me even more than the divorce. He went to live with a relative, but things only got worse. For example, try to imagine what it was like for me, a mother, to pick up the *Washington Post* on a Mother's Day morning and see a front page article on homeless people panhandling, with an accompanying picture of my son, identified by name. Heartbreaking!

Soon after my husband's announcement, I realized I had to pull myself together for my children and for myself. In those days, a woman's employment options were basically to be a secretary, a teacher or a nurse. Despite the fact that I had no desire to be a nurse, I enrolled in a nursing program and graduated as an R.N. Two days before I was to start a job in an adolescent rehab unit, I stepped off a curb and ruptured a disc in my back. This laid me up for over a year. Somehow, again, by the grace of God, I always managed to see the humor in situations and this saved me. I didn't need to watch soap operas—I was starring in one!

At one point, I had three jobs for a total annual salary of $6,000. Life was difficult, but also joyous, sharing special times with my boys, my parents and my friends and co-workers. After my two younger sons graduated from high school, I accepted a job at a Catholic high school for boys, first in Development, then as the Director of Retreats, co-facilitator of support groups and filling in when they needed to say they had a school nurse. I experienced twenty wonderful, fulfilling years there.

Somewhere along the way I began to feel the anger the marriage counselor had alluded to long ago and became less forgiving. Selfishly, it often bothers me that my former husband has, in recent years, turned up (with his fourth wife) as the so-called "benevolent father/grandfather." On various family occasions, I have to be in his company, and it is not always easy. I try to be forgiving, but I have difficulty when I recall some of the terrible things he did, harming me and our sons emotionally. I pray daily for the gift of completely forgiving him and sincerely hope that someday I will succeed. It is definitely a challenge.

— Mary Ellen Whitcomb

— Proverbs 16:24 —

Kindly words are a honeycomb,

sweet to the taste, wholesome to the body.

Reconciliation

— Psalm 51 —

Have mercy upon me, O God, according to thy loving
kindness: according unto the multitude of thy
tender mercies blot out my transgressions.

Wash me throughly from mine iniquity, and cleanse
me from my sin.

For I acknowledge my transgressions: and my sin is
ever before me.

Against thee, thee only, have I sinned, and done this
evil in thy sight: that thou mightest be justified
when thou speakest, and be clear when thou
judgest.

Behold, I was shapen in iniquity; and in sin did my
mother conceive me.

Behold, thou desirest truth in the inward parts: and
in the hidden part thou shalt make me to know
wisdom.

Purge me with hyssop, and I shall be clean: wash me,
and I shall be whiter than snow.

Make me to hear joy and gladness; that the bones which thou hast broken may rejoice.

Hide thy face from my sins, and blot out all mine iniquities.

Create in me a clean heart, O God; and renew a right spirit within me.

Cast me not away from thy presence; and take not thy holy spirit from me.

Restore unto me the joy of thy salvation; and uphold me with thy free spirit.

Then will I teach transgressors thy ways; and sinners shall be converted unto thee.

— A Litany for Reconciliation and Renewal —

from *Psalm 51*

Have mercy on me, O God, according to your
steadfast love;
according to your abundant mercy blot out my
transgressions.

*Create in me a clean heart, O God, and put a new and
right spirit within me.*

Wash me thoroughly from my iniquity, and cleanse
me from my sin.

For I know my transgressions, and my sin is ever
before me.

*Create in me a clean heart, O God, and put a new and
right spirit within me.*

You desire truth in the inward being; therefore teach
me wisdom in my secret heart.

*Create in me a clean heart, O God, and put a new and
right spirit within me.*

Purge me with hyssop, and I shall be clean; wash me,
and I shall be whiter than snow.

*Create in me a clean heart, O God, and put a new and
right spirit within me.*

Let me hear joy and gladness; let the bones that you have crushed rejoice.

Create in me a clean heart, O God, and put a new and right spirit within me.

Restore to me the joy of your salvation, and sustain in me a willing spirit.

Create in me a clean heart, O God, and put a new and right spirit within me.

O God, O God of my salvation,... my tongue will sing aloud of your deliverance.
O Lord, open my lips, and my mouth will declare your praise.

Create in me a clean heart, O God, and put a new and right spirit within me.

The Lord Jesus, raised up on the cross, drew everything to himself.
Let us proclaim his greatness and pray to him:

Lord, draw all things to yourself.

Lord, may all be drawn to the light that shines from the mystery of your cross:
let it show them you are the Way, the Truth, and the Life.

Lord, draw all things to yourself.

To all that thirst, give the water of life:
    let them not be thirsty forever.

Lord, draw all things to yourself.

May we who seek you in trust and faith,
    in hopeful prayer and in patient waiting, be found
    by you.

Lord, draw all things to yourself.

Twenty-seven years have gone by, and I can vividly remember how I felt crouching behind a rock about a toddler's height. Behind the rock, afraid but still I held my toddling brother Bessi close to my side. My dog, Whiskey, was beside watching keenly but with an unusual stillness of a dog. He may have saved our life that day.

What really happened? It was a sunny morning. I was at home, at least what became home since it was a temporary habitation. We had fled our real home due to the fighting in the north of Uganda in 1980–1981. We came to this home to escape being killed.

That sunny morning, while I was at home and going about the ordinary chores cleaning the compound. After having milked the cows, there was a loud deafening sound. It was strange and yet a familiar sound. I had heard that sound many times before. Only this time it was too close. I had only half a minute to rush inside the house and grab little Bessi. Whiskey followed me.

I turned around to see if my other brother and sisters had a chance to escape the invasion. I saw none of them. At a distance about 500 meters, soldiers were rampaging through the abandoned camp. Some were pursuing chickens while others kicked doors entering in and out, picking what ever interested them. There was really nothing much to steal from the poor. It was not things that brought us there. We wanted to protect our lives.

After the raid that lasted a good ten minutes, we saw the soldiers leaving in a single file. I could see they were heading toward the rock that has become our temporary shelter. Whiskey raised up his ears, his tail tense. It looked like it was now his turn to attack. I held my breath, put my hand across Bessi's face to hide him from what was to befall us: in a moment of magnificent show of power and victory from the rock. Only God could have done that. The file of soldiers heading toward the rock took a turn abruptly and walked away. I was seized by fear and trembling. Whiskey was trembling too. We got up, walked towards the river—not knowing where we were going—just walking away. My knees felt weak and could hardly carry me along. Perhaps someone was carrying us. Anyway, I have, over the years been carried, and this is my Rock.

After crossing the River Ayoo, we walked further ahead and there we met the people of the village who had gathered at the foot of a large rock. They were hungry and tired from running and hiding. When we appeared, there was a momentary panic obviously some thought we were the government soldiers. I called out to them. It is me I said, do not run away. My voice was recognized and they stopped. All were elated to see three of us. The fear and the anxiety that had gripped them were transformed into cries of joy and praise. God is great! Oh God!

— Issac Kiyaka, S.J.
Niarobi, Kenya

── Chicken Casserole ──

2 cups cooked chicken

2 cans cream of chicken soup

½ cup mayonnaise

2 cups diced celery

2 cups cooked rice

2 tsps grated onion

2 tbls lemon juice

1 tsp salt

1 cup slivered almonds

2 sups buttered crushed cornflakes

Mix all except almonds and cornflakes. Place in large casserole dish or two 8 x 10" Pyrex (oven safe) dishes. Sprinkle with almonds and cornflakes. Bake at 375° for 30 minutes.

Serves 8

— Ann Brown

September 11, 2001

When I kept silence, my bones waxed old through my roaring all the day long.

For day and night thy hand was heavy upon me: my moisture is turned into the drought of summer.

I acknowledge my sin unto thee, and mine iniquity have I not hid. I said, I will confess my transgressions unto the Lord; and thou forgavest the iniquity of my sin.

For this shall every one that is godly pray unto thee in a time when thou mayest be found: surely in the floods of great waters they shall not come nigh unto him.

Thou art my hiding place; thou shalt preserve me from trouble; thou shalt compass me about with songs of deliverance.

I will instruct thee and teach thee in the way which thou shalt go: I will guide thee with mine eye.

Be ye not as the horse, or as the mule, which have no understanding: whose mouth must be held in with bit and bridle, lest they come near unto thee.

Many sorrows shall be to the wicked: but he that trusteth in the Lord, mercy shall compass him about.

Be glad in the Lord, and rejoice, ye righteous: and shout for joy, all ye that are upright in heart.

September 13th I found myself facing a classroom of students stunned, looking at me without any sense of hope or future. I myself wasn't sure how to begin to address the meaning of that day. So I stood there praying to the Holy Spirit, asking for guidance and thought to myself that one thing I can do is talk about the three times in my own life that were similar to that day.

So I told them about Friday, November 22nd, 1963– the day that John F. Kennedy was assassinated. No reaction. Then I talked very personally about a very difficult time in my own life– the day I came home from work on a hot August day with a letter waiting to tell me whether or not I would be drafted to go to Viet Nam. No reaction. The third, when I did get some reaction, was when I told them about the afternoon I met with a doctor who told me that I had cancer, and would be having surgery immediately that evening, and no guarantees. That did get a bit of a reaction, but still not enough to get a conversation going.

So then I thought for a minute and what I could do was ask everybody to take a minute to be quiet. We did so and then I asked the students to tell me what emotion was going through their minds and their hearts at that moment. As we registered those emotions I realized that

I had a real challenge. Emotions ranged from anger to fear to hatred to despair.

Finally one young junior said very quietly, "Father, I will never bring children into this world. I will never put anybody through what we are going through right now." That's when I knew that I had to say something. So I said, "This is your homework assignment and I want you to begin it now and take it home and bring it back next class. I want you to sit down and write a letter to your son or daughter, talking about the meaning of September 11th in your own life. And I want you to pour out your emotions and all the things that are going through you right now. And I want you to record them for your own children."

It kind of stunned them for a minute, but I realized it did shake them back into some reality, possibly that the world would go on. When I returned two days later to receive these letters, I'll never forget the letter I received from one student, an ROTC freshman, who wrote the letter that I pray all of us could write about our lives and our world that day. He talked about faith, he talked about peace, he talked about justice, and he called on the meaning of the power of Martin Luther King, Jr., who said, "We cannot allow this kind of hatred to consume us. We must move forward in peace." I knew then that the Holy Spirit was with us.

— A College Student Reflects —

Patriotism has been put on its highest pedestal this past week following the terrorist attack on the World Trade Center. The nation as a whole has been brought together in a common cause. It is hard for me to look at the front page of the *New York Times* today, September 17, 2001, and see the New York City skyline missing those two great towers. The nation-wide feeling right now cannot be described in words. No one knows what to call it, but everyone feels the same thing, regardless of ethnicity. The main thing to strive for in a time like this is justice, not prejudice. This tragic event hit everyone hard, but American resolve will come back stronger than ever. Although one cannot escape his emotions, one must not give into them or let them skew the clarity of logic. I can do nothing but sympathize with Mayor Guiliani's crying photo on the *Time*'s front page. It has been one of the hardest things for me in order to hold back the tears. The most important thing is to have faith that this beautiful country will succeed in pulling through such a tragedy.

One tough question that plagues humanity is "What do we live for?" Many people have different answers, and for now mine is still not definite. Martin

Luther King, Jr. said that to live, you must have something to die for. Right now, for me, that answer is spread across many things, primarily my family. I do know the answer will become clear as soon as one thing happens—I get a family of my own and raise children. The one thing I want most for my children is for them to live in a world free from fear. That is, a world where they have no reason to fear their lives. Although the emotion of fear is negative, it should also not be absent. Once my children arrive on this earth, I know my sole purpose in life will be for their long-term happiness. God willing this prediction will come true in its most sincere culmination.

— Michael Joseph Lettieri
my former student
September 14, 2001

— Mike Canty's Service —

Perhaps the most important thing that Mike ever taught me was to not hate.

It seems simple enough, perhaps even common sense, but growing up in the 80's, the word 'hate' became a word that many of us said without really putting much thought behind the meaning of. Things like "I *hate* asparagus", or "I *hate* calculus" or maybe today "I *hate* the Arizona Diamondbacks" seemed to roll off our tongues all too casually.

Mike taught me not to hate one afternoon back at Loyola. It seems that someone had really gotten under my skin, I returned to the dorm looking for someone to commiserate with and found Mike...probably doing a crossword. "Nah, I don't hate anyone." Clearly, not the response I was going for. I tried to persuade him over to my side, the dark side, telling him the story of how she had irritated me to see if he would join in my tirade. All he would say was "Well, yeah, I guess that's pretty bad and she's probably not a very nice person, but you shouldn't *hate* anyone."

That has stayed with me for almost ten years. And now more than ever it's time that we believe what Mike would believe, as hard as it might be, and for us to not hate right now.

> — Memorial Mass for Mike Canty,
> my former student
> St. Ignatius Church, NYC

Excerpts From Sermons Across the Nation
The New York Times, Monday September 17, 2001

MAPLEWOOD, NJ
The Rev. Rick Boyer
Prospect Presbyterian Church
"God stands with us, weeps with us, strengthens us, mourns with us."

MANHATTAN
Rabbi J. Rolando Matalon
Congregation B'nai Jeshurun
"And what do we do for peace? It is a time for questions. To sit with reflection.

"We must be extremely careful. And, careful with ourselves. So it doesn't turn into resentment. We have many things to do and think about. Now, we do this: just sit together."

BROOKLYN
Bonnie Myotai Treace, Sensei
Fire Lotus Temple, Zen Mountain Monastery
"Thousands of blossoms, red, brown, white, yellow, black scattered on ground made tender by their falling."

This human body, more fragile than the dew drops on the countless tips of morning grass."

"My wailing voice is the bright September wind and in the dark night, silence speaks:

"I will die only when love dies and you will not let love die."

BROOKLYN
The Rev. Vladimir Alexeev
Holy Trinity Orthodox Church

"The terrorist and all who stand behind them thought they'll win, but they failed. From the devastated buildings and the crashing airplanes, people cried the most important words they could find. They're the words of love. Love can't fail. Love always wins.

"Today is a day of sorrow, but today is also the day of victory of love. These people who died by the terrorist attack aren't victims, they're heroes. They're heroes of love and true humanity. We want them to hear us: We love you, too!"

SOUTH BARRINGTON, IL
The Rev. Bill Hybels
Willow Creek Community Church

"I will never look at a firefighter the same way again. What is in someone, hundreds of them, to compel them to run into a burning building while everyone else is running out, just to save people they don't even know? Their bravery has become part of our collective legacy. Their bravery dignifies us all.

MANHASSET, NY
The Rev. Edward Corley
Mount Olive Baptist Church

"We share a commonality, irrespective of race, creed or color. We have the same blood, the same heartbeat. So Lord, somehow our destinies are intertwined. So if there are ways that we can reach out, and alleviate the heartbreaks, whatever way, Lord, give us the courage.

LAWRENCEVILLE, NJ
The Rev. H. Dana Fearon 3rd
The Presbyterian Church of Lawrenceville

"In the midst of the tragedy of Tuesday, Jesus Christ came to walk over the chaos. The passengers of the plane that crashed outside Pittsburgh knew they were going to die, and they took a vote, which was unanimous, and rushed the terrorists to take the plane down before it could reach its target. They did better than Peter did when Jesus told him that he, too, could walk over the chaos."

BROOKLYN

The Rev. Gregory Stankus

St. Francis Xavier Roman Catholic Church

"It is so important today, in our sorrow in our loss, that we seek to create and to rebuild, not just our buildings, but rebuild our hearts and our society. That we call upon the mercy of God to lift us up again, make us new by knowing that we are weak, by knowing that we are frail and we need. By knowing that what we build is not strong enough, by knowing that if only we pay attention to the people on our sidewalks, that if only we pay attention to the people in need during the good times, can we say that we are building Christ's Kingdom."

SAN FRANCISCO

The Very Rev. Alan Jones

Grace Episcopal Cathedral

"These great and terrible events present us with choice. We can choose the downward spiral of despair and resentment and the cry of vengeance, or we can choose a better way even as we work for justice. That better way is the way of the peace of God which passes all understanding. God's peace, God's shalom, God's salaam. God's peace is not weak or passive. It is not peace at any price. God's shalom, salaam, peace is active, arduous and passionate. It is about wholeness and integrity, justice and mercy, inclusion and human flourishing.

"It is a free gift yet it is something we have to freely accept and make our own. We have to choose— choose love over fear."

MANASQUAN, NJ
The Rev. William J. Bausch
Chapel, Church of St. Denis

"Finally, we must turn to the bereaved. Comfort them. And here, let me give you this advice. Don't worry about words. As I said to one man who has lost a son, 'I usually have no trouble with words. They come easily. But now I find that I am at a loss as to what to say to you in your pain. But if I can't offer words, what I can do is offer you two shoulders to cry on and my simple presence of being here with you in your time of grief.' And he said, 'That's enough.' And it is.

"Turn to God, turn to one another, turn to the bereaved."

Lord, make me an instrument of your peace:
    Where there is hatred, let me sow love;
    Where there is injury, pardon;
    Where there is doubt, faith;
    Where there is despair, hope;
    Where there is darkness, light;
    And where there is sadness, joy.

O Divine Master, grant that I may not so much seek
    To be consoled as to console,
    To be understood as to understand,
    To be loved as to love.

For it is in giving that we receive,
    It is in pardoning that we are pardoned,
    And it is in dying that we are born to eternal
    life.

— St. Francis of Assisi

— I am the Great Sun —

From a Normandy Crucifix of 1632.

I am the great sun, but you do not see me,
I am your husband, but you turn away.
I am the captive, but you do not free me,
I am the captain you will not obey.

I am the truth, but you will not believe me,
I am the city, where you will not stay.
I am your wife, your child, but you will leave me,
I am the God to whom you will not pray.

I am your counsel, but you do not hear me,
I am the lover whom you will betray.
I am the victor, but you do not cheer me,
I am the holy dove whom you will slay.

I am your life, but you will not name me,
Seal up your soul with tears and do not blame me.

— Charles Causley

Compassion

—Psalm 121—

I will lift up mine eyes unto the hills, from whence cometh my help.

help cometh from the Lord, which made heaven and earth.

He will not suffer thy foot to be moved: he that keepeth thee will not slumber.

Behold, he that keepeth Israel shall neither slumber nor sleep.

The Lord is thy keeper: the Lord is thy shade upon thy right hand.

The sun shall not smite thee by day, nor the moon by night.

The Lord shall preserve thee from all evil: he shall preserve thy soul.

The Lord shall preserve thy going out and thy coming in from this time forth, and even for evermore.

— Compassion —

Recently I heard a story that expressed the meaning of compassion and forgiveness better than any explanation I had ever heard before. Let me start today by telling you this tale.

Once there was a very old man who used to meditate early every morning under a large tree on the bank of the Ganges River in India. One morning, having finished his meditation, the old man opened his eyes and saw a scorpion floating helplessly in the strong current of the river. As the scorpion was pulled closer to the tree, it got caught in the long tree roots that branched out far into the river. The scorpion struggled frantically to free itself but got more and more entangled in the complex network of the tree roots.

When the old man saw this, he immediately stretched himself onto the extended roots and reached out to rescue the drowning scorpion. But as soon as he touched it, the animal jerked and stung him wildly. Instinctively, the man withdrew his hand, but then after regaining his balance, he once again stretched himself out along the roots to save the agonized scorpion. But every time the old man came within reach the scorpion stung him so badly with its poisonous tail that his hands became swollen and bloody and his face distorted by pain.

At that moment, a passer-by saw the old man stretched out on the roots struggling with the scorpion and shouted: "Hey, stupid old man. What's wrong with you? Only a fool risks his life for the sake of an ugly, useless creature. Don't you know that you may kill yourself to save that ungrateful animal?"

Slowly the old man turned his head, and looking calmly in the stranger's eyes, he said: "Friend, because it is the nature of the scorpion to sting, why should I give up my own nature to save?"

— As told by Henri Nouwen

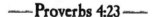

Proverbs 4:23

More than all else, keep watch over your heart,

since here are the wellsprings of life.

—Training Service Dogs While in Prison—

This story is about a great program I am involved in called **Canine Partners For Life** (CPL). The program has prisoners volunteering to train dogs for people with disabilities. These dogs are trained for 2 years— one year in here by us (prisoners) and one year back in Pennsylvania (CPL training facility). Then if they meet the qualifications they will be placed with someone who has a disability. CPL provides an array of service dogs, including seizure alert and diabetic alert dogs. General Service Dogs provide a multitude of tasks for people who are disabled. They can retrieve items from all over the house including food, medicine, and drinks. They can also open and close

doors, drawers and refrigerators. They assist people in wheelchairs, help stabilize those with mild walking and balance disorders, and assist those with low energy syndromes. I can only imagine how much these dogs improve someone's quality of life when they are placed with them.

I would like to give you my perspective on being involved in the program. There is one dog and two people per cell. Both people are dog handlers and share all the responsibilities of the dog. There is a large dog kennel in the cell which makes things pretty cramped. At this time there are four dogs and eight handlers in the program. When we train we try to work together as a group and sometimes switch dogs to ensure the dogs are able to follow the commands given by any of the handlers.

After an interview and evaluation I was accepted into the program on April 11, 2013, so I'm still somewhat new. When I started the dogs were almost a year old and on their way out so they knew all the commands already. Basically I was the one receiving the training by other senior handlers on how to train the dogs. Plus I had a really well trained dog, Savoy, which made it easier to learn. This actually worked out really well because it gave me some training and experience for when the new puppies came. On June

30, 2013, our fully trained dogs left and the puppies (8 weeks old) arrived.

My training with my first dog was a good learning experience. After only one week in the program I was able to start taking him to work with me in the school where I am a tutor and other places as well. I was somewhat nervous at first because I had never walked a dog on the leash with me anywhere, even when I was home. After a few days I got used to it though and after a few weeks I really enjoyed having Savoy with me everywhere I went. It was even to the point that on the days my cellmate wanted to keep him I was a little sad; it just wasn't the same going to work without Savoy. I even took a few pictures with him. Even though my time with him was short (less than 3 months), it was special and I will never forget him. I hope he makes it to become a service dog and is partnered with someone that loves him and is truly uplifted and benefits from his companionship and assistance.

On the day the new puppy "Hector" came I decided I was going to put on a tough-guy façade because I knew he would also be leaving me in a year, and I didn't want to get too attached. So when they came my cell buddy picked out Hector and played with him a few minutes, then he handed him to me and immediately all the toughness melted away. I felt a bond and connection right away. It was something I hadn't felt in a long, long time.

I've only had Hector a short time now, and even though I don't have children, this is the only thing I know to compare it with. It is a big responsibility. My sleep has definitely suffered and it takes a lot of patience. Other trainers have been telling me how rigorous this training is, and I wasn't really seeing it until a few days ago. That's the first day we tried to get Hector to walk up the steps; he only walked up two. The next day I was by myself and I got him to walk up the entire flight of steps and walk on the grates (which sometimes the dogs don't like to do). I was so happy! I could actually see the results. I could also see that Hector trusted me and a real close bond was forming.

Over the past few weeks Hector and I have really bonded and he is progressing very quickly. He has learned all of his Level I commands. The second week we had him, my cell partner left the program and I had to handle all the responsibilities by myself, all the feedings, bathroom excursions, cleaning, etc. It was a lot of work and it took a week before they moved in another handler. I am very proud of Hector for his progress and myself for my commitment and dedication to him. Although I haven't been in this program very long I can see it is producing change in me. Prison has made me feel *disconnected* in so many ways, but I'm beginning to feel connected again. It's truly a blessing to be involved in this great program. Being committed to this program will change someone's life and I thank God I'm able to recognize how it has changing me.

I am really looking forward to this year I will be spending with Hector. I am excited to see what the results of my/our hard work will be. I know at times it won't be easy, but I must always remember why I'm doing this—to give back to the community and hopefully help someone who needs it and that their lives will be changed and benefited by their *Canine Partner For Life*.

— Joshua Cahall
Jessup Correctional Institution

This

year,

end a quarrel.

Seek out a forgotten

friend. Dismiss suspicion,

and replace it with trust...

Write a love letter. Share some

treasure. Give a soft answer. En-

courage youth. Manifest your loyalty in

word and deed. Keep a promise. Find the

time. Forget a grudge. Forgive an enemy. Listen.

Apologize if you are wrong. Try to understand.

Flout envy. Examine your demands on others. Think

first of someone else. Appreciate. Be kind. Be gentle.

Laugh a little. Laugh a little more. Deserve confidence.

Take up arms against malice. Decry complacency. Express

your gratitude. Go to church. Welcome a stranger. Gladden

the heart of a child. Take pleasure in the beauty and

wonder of the earth. Speak

your love. Speak

it again. Speak

it still once

again.

Forgiveness

O Lord God of my salvation, I have cried day *and* night before thee:

Let my prayer come before thee: incline thine ear unto my cry;

For my soul is full of troubles: and my life draweth nigh unto the grave.

I am counted with them that go down into the pit: I am as a man *that hath* no strength:

Free among the dead, like the slain that lie in the grave, whom thou rememberest no more: and they are cut off from thy hand.

Thou hast laid me in the lowest pit, in darkness, in the deeps.

Thy wrath lieth hard upon me, and thou hast afflicted *me* with all thy waves.

Thou hast put away mine acquaintance far from me; thou hast made me an abomination unto them: *I am* shut up, and I cannot come forth.

Mine eye mourneth by reason of affliction: Lord, I have called daily upon thee, I have stretched out my hands unto thee.

Wilt thou shew wonders to the dead? shall the dead arise *and* praise thee?

Shall thy lovingkindness be declared in the grave? *or* thy faithfulness in destruction?

Shall thy wonders be known in the dark? and thy righteousness in the land of forgetfulness?

But unto thee have I cried, O Lord; and in the morning shall my prayer prevent thee.

Lord, why castest thou off my soul? *why* hidest thou thy face from me?

I *am* afflicted and ready to die from *my* youth up: *while* I suffer thy terrors I am distracted.

Thy fierce wrath goeth over me; thy terrors have cut me off.

They came round about me daily like water; they compassed me about together.

Lover and friend hast thou put far from me, *and* mine acquaintance into darkness.

To some, the notion of forgiveness might be a little like gratitude – a happy rainbow concept that seems to fade as soon as it appears. The definition might be clear but the practical application is not. To others, forgiveness is as profound and necessary as the water that rains from the sky: it is tangible, nourishing and real. It is not a concept to be contemplated and understood as much as it is an action to be taken. Earning forgiveness can be a wholly transformative act that can unite the offender, the victim, and God. Despite the popularity of the Lord's Prayer it is not certain what was meant by the petition in Matthew 6:12 to "forgive us our trespasses" as we "forgive those who trespass against us." The word "trespasses" was a translation for the word "debt," in the Greek to mean sins or offenses, but some scholars believe that "debt" was the intended meaning. "Trespasses" could very well mean sinful offenses, but given the historical context of Caesar's taxation policies and Roman landowners feeling burdened, many believe the word was intended to reflect a financial debt and something owed. *Forgive us our debts as we forgive those who debt against us.* This would make sense since Christ's teachings emphasized obedience to God and not to the law. *Give to Caesar what is Caesar's and give to God what is God's.* If the word "debt" was the intended meaning, then it changes the context of forgiveness from something elusive to something very practical.

One of the more publicized and practical stories of forgiveness is that of the 2006 school shooting in the Amish community of Nickel Mines, Pennsylvania. The tragedy took place when a distraught local deliveryman took control of a small schoolhouse, killed five little girls execution style, seriously injured five more, and then killed himself. The shooting was a major international news story, but in the days afterwards, another story emerged about how the Amish community and the parents of the girls openly forgave the killer and his family. Hundreds of news accounts appeared in the media when reporters observed the Amish families and friends of the slayed girls attending the burial of the killer, reaching out to comfort, embrace, feed and even donate money to the killer's widow and his children. Many of the Amish spoke of their forgiveness toward the killer almost immediately after the killings.

Researchers studying the Amish at that time wrote a book called *Amish Grace* about the shooting and the story of their forgiveness toward the killer. In it, they define forgiveness as what happens when "a victim forgoes the right to revenge and commits to overcoming bitter feelings toward the wrongdoer." They define "reconciliation" as the act of restoring and healing the relationship between victim and offender following the offense. Instead of forgiveness as something fleeting, it is solid.

The researchers explained that Amish considered forgiveness a normal part of their living, arising from their deep faith in Christ. While the world expressed amazement about the Amish 'forgiveness story," the Amish expressed surprise by the world's reaction to their forgiveness. Members of the Amish community could not understand why anyone was surprised. They said that to forgive the killer was "just standard Christian forgiveness." It was a "natural, spontaneous and quite ordinary thing" made possible through God's grace.

Certainly not everyone can see things this way. Most of us feel that the injustices done to us – the abuse, the crimes, the hurts – are simply too great to let go of. And perhaps we just don't want to forgo our right to revenge and prefer to hold onto the bitterness as a means of subtle or overt punishment toward our offenders. It works the opposite way as well: when we are the offenders and have committed something we think is awful, we feel so bad we don't want to forgive ourselves. Forget about God, we'll be the judge. We punish ourselves and hold onto our remorse.

For a recovering alcoholic who is coming to terms with a drunken past, self blame and remorse can be deadly. The AA program recognizes the necessity for self-forgiveness and reconciliation. That is why the Twelve Steps ask the alcoholic to reflect on their lives as problem drinkers, look at the harms they have caused themselves and others, ask for God's help and begin the process of repairing their relationships. Once they have recognized and admitted the nature of their wrongdoings as alcoholics, they can begin to right those wrongs. This happens through the practice of the Eighth and Ninth steps when they write a list of all the persons they have harmed (Step Eight) and "made direct amends" to those people they have harmed wherever possible. (Step Nine)

The book *Alcoholics Anonymous* explains that most alcoholics don't look forward to this step. These steps are not meant to be easy; they are meant to release the alcoholic from their sense of guilt by making them accountable and responsible. The Ninth Step encourages the alcoholic not just to admit to past transgressions, but to make financial amends as well (meaning take out the check book). This could entail having to go back to a previous employer to admit that they stole money from the company or took unauthorized time off. It could require facing their children and trying to make up for missing all those sports games because of their drinking. By taking action, they will not be haunted by their past in such a way as to make them want to drink again.

But the Ninth Step is not really about forgiveness. Forgiveness might be a positive outcome of re-paying a family member for money "borrowed" or goods damaged, because in many cases forgiveness will not happen. The alcoholic's random acts of intoxication just won't be forgivable by everyone. Some parents won't be able to make up for the damage done to their kids. Some spouses will not get past an alcoholic's years of rage or absenteeism. The good news is that most alcoholics find that the people they harmed are very receptive to their amends. The offer of sincerely trying to amend what went wrong opens a door for healing and reconciliation. And, in *all cases* the alcoholic will be able to be freed from past bad behaviors by taking tangible, meaningful action.

Not unlike the Amish who attributed their ability to forgive to God's divine grace, the alcoholic is only able to make amends and reconcile their relationships through humility. Humility is a requirement for being able to see that offenses were committed, admit to them, and then work to fix the harms done. This can only happen when the alcoholic has found a Higher Power and can set aside ego long enough to see the truth about the past and take action to make it better. It is not enough to know that harms were done and not act.

What is so powerful about the Ninth Step amends process is that it enables forgiveness to come from those who have been harmed, clears a foundation for self-forgiveness and makes it possible for forgiveness from God. Having the humility to see ourselves as fallible or weakened by addiction, as children of God, removes the need to hold on to guilt, shame and bitterness. Humbly admitting to our transgressions by voicing them to another defuses their power over us and lessens our need to hold onto them. Similarly, speaking about the harms done to us, can be equally freeing. Through humble action, the grace of God makes it possible for self-forgiveness, forgiveness from others and forgiveness from God.

Krayhill, Donald B, Nolt, Steven M. and Weaver-Zercher David L., *Amish Grace: How Forgiveness Transcended Tragedy*, San Francisco: John Wiley & Sons, 2007.

Perrotta, Kevin. *The Our Father*, Chicago: Loyola Press, 2007.

Alcoholics Anonymous, Alcoholics Anonymous World Services: New York, 2001.

— Kathryn Burns

1. We admitted we were powerless over alcohol—
   that our lives had become unmanageable.

2. Came to believe that a Power greater than
   ourselves could restore us to sanity.

3. Made a decision to turn our will and our lives
   over to the care of God *as we understood Him.*

4. Made a searching and fearless moral inventory of
   ourselves.

5. Admitted to God, to ourselves, and to another
   human being the exact nature of our wrongs.

6. Were entirely ready to have God remove all these
   defects of character.

7. Humbly asked Him to remove our shortcomings.

8. Made a list of all persons we had harmed, and
   became willing to make amends to them all.

9. Made direct amends to such people wherever
   possible, except when to do so would injure them
   or others.

10. Continued to take personal inventory and when
    we were wrong promptly admitted it.

11. Sought through prayer and meditation to improve our conscious contact with God, *as we understood Him*, praying only for knowledge of His will for us and the power to carry that out.

12. Having had a spiritual awakening as the result of these Steps, we tried to carry this message to alcoholics, and to practice these principles in all our affairs.

——Forgiveness——

Matthew 18: 21–22

How often must I forgive my brother or sister?

Seven times?

and Jesus answered not seven times but 70 times seven times.

—Letting Go—

To "let go" does not mean to stop caring, it means I can't do it for someone else.

To "let go" is not to cut myself off, it's the realization I can't control another.

To "let go" is not to enable, but to allow learning from natural consequences.

To "let go" is to admit powerlessness, which means the outcome is not in my hands.

To "let go" is not to try to change or blame another, it's to make the most of myself.

To "let go" is not to care for, but care about.

To "let go" is not to fix, but to be supportive.

To "let go" is not to judge, but to allow another to be a human being.

To "let go" is not to be in the middle arranging all the outcomes, but to allow others to affect their own destinies.

To "let go" is not to be protective, it's to permit another to face reality.

To "let go" is not to deny, but to accept.

To "let go" is not to nag, scold or argue, but instead to search out my own shortcoming and correct them.

To "let go" is not to adjust everything to my desires but to take each day as it comes, and cherish myself in it.

To "let go" is not to regret the past, but to grow and live for the future.

To "let go" is to fear less and love more..."

— Author Unknown

Forgiveness is the largest spiritual and philosophical question that challenges me. It shamelessly reveals my tendency toward hypocrisy. On the one hand, I seek forgiveness for the many wrongs that I've committed. While one the other hand, I find it quite difficult to forgive the wrongs that have been committed against me. I often tell myself that there are some acts for which there can be no expiation— no forgiveness. Of course, if I accept that there are some acts for which forgiveness is not possible, then I condemn myself to a psychological hell.

Experience has shown me time and time again that when I offer genuine forgiveness for a wrong committed against me, I almost immediately experience a lightness and joy in my own heart and soul. Whenever I hold on to those contemptuous feelings I experience when I feel that someone has wronged me, I ache with anger until I can exact revenge. I get a tightness in my stomach; my stress level soars and my passions rage out of control when I come into contact with someone I feel has wronged me. My normal ability to reason and to maintain good continence disappears. When I interpret some act committed against me to be a wrong or some kind of slight, an anger engulfs me that knocks me off balance—and I'm not able to find my balance, my equilibrium, until I forgive the person, people, or act itself that so angered me.

I can't deny the transformative effect that forgiveness affords me. But still, I often find it difficult to indiscriminately extend forgiveness. I wonder if my inclination to hold onto some anger makes me some kind of masochist. There are times when someone wrongs me, and he doesn't even know that he did. It wasn't a malicious intent that injured my ego, my pride—or whatever. It was simply my interpretation of the matter that rendered me disturbed—or angry. I understand this in a profound way.

Long ago, I learned about an ABC system: "A" stands for activating event, "B" stands for belief system, and "C" is for emotional consequence. "A" never causes "C," the emotional consequence. "B" causes or directly leads to "C." In short, our belief about an activating event ("A") is what causes our emotional consequence ("C") —our feelings. For instance, if someone steals my watch, and I become angry about the thief, it's not the stealing of my watch, per se, that has me angry. It's my belief that I own the watch; it's my personal property and no one is supposed to take it without my permission that has me angry.

If I were to renounce ownership of all personal property, and declare all things in my possession a matter of community property, then I would not likely be angered by the thief of anything. My belief system wouldn't allow for it.

Alas, I've come to realize that anger—which gives birth to hatred, resentment, and bitterness will eat through and completely destroy any human heart and soul that tries to contain them. We humans are vibratory creatures. We all desire to be accepted, loved, cared for, and cared about. But when we allow anger to overwhelm us and infuse us with hatred, resentment, and bitterness we inadvertently push away from ourselves the very things we most desire: to be loved and accepted... No one wants to be around a hateful and bitter person.

Every person born and bred to live will face instances in his or her life when he or she feels justified in hating someone or something for a transgression. You may find it extremely difficult, hell, damn near impossible to forgive some very diabolical and base acts. But I assure you, when you do genuinely forgive, a huge weight is lifted from your soul.

When you're not hating someone or anyone for any reason whatsoever—and you're not harboring any resentment and bitterness—you'll radiate such a warm and wonderful aura you'll attract to yourself all the love and acceptance you'll ever need to aid you through life. For the human journey is fraught with hardships and suffering. So much so, we all need forgiveness to survive.

"Forgive us of our debt as we forgive our debtors," Jesus teaches us. It's a powerful lesson. If we embrace it, the path we choose in life will be much easier to journey. When someone wrongs you, whether in a real or imagined way, summon the courage to genuinely forgive that person—not for his or her sake—but your own. The adrenalin that courses through your body and creates an assortment of physiological stresses is far more injurious to you than the person, people, or thing you're angry at. The damage done to the human soul because of an inability or unwillingness to forgive is immeasurable. But the experience of lightness and joy realized from genuinely forgiving is grandly ineffable.

I'm intimately aware of how cruel man can be toward others. I've committed treacherous acts toward my fellow man and treacherous acts have been committed against me. I salute Joseph Conrad for eloquently declaring, "Man alone is cruel." Man is the only animal in God's creation that inflicts pain and injury for the sheer pleasure of it.

I've had close family members robbed and murdered. I've seen people physically tortured. I've seen murder and rape up-close and in very personal ways. I came of age on the ghetto streets and in the Maryland Penitentiary. It's easy for me to focus on the acts that the genteel of society would find barbaric and evil—and not worthy of forgiveness. But, for the sake of my own soul and psychological comfort, I have forgiven the perfidious, evil, and treacherous acts committed against me. And, likewise, I hope that the perfidious, evil, and treacherous acts I've committed have been forgiven.

I face a great number of small, petty, nuisance stuff. But no one or nothing is big enough or significant enough to make me hate. I stand on the principle of forgiveness not because I'm some grand magnanimous person. I stand on it because I'm small and insignificant. Forgiveness simply props me up and carry me along my arduous journey sans the burden of hatred, resentment, and bitterness.

— Arlando "Tray" Jones III
Jessup Correctional Institution

—Conclusion—

I hear and I forget
I see and I react
I do and I understand

Only God can make it
possible for me to forgive

Divine action
Joint cooperation
Not my initiative.

No.

The Holy Spirit's work

To forgive
Never passive
Always active

Let go

Let go

Accept the fact that
I am a loved sinner

Talented writers, innovative students, fresh minds at work.

Apprentice House is the country's only campus-based, student-staffed book publishing company. Directed by professors and industry professionals, it is a nonprofit activity of the Communication Department at Loyola University Maryland.

Using state-of-the-art technology and an experiential learning model of education, Apprentice House publishes books in untraditional ways. This dual responsibility as publishers and educators creates an unprecedented collaborative environment among faculty and students, while teaching tomorrow's editors, designers, and marketers.

Outside of class, progress on book projects is carried forth by the AH Book Publishing Club, a co-curricular campus organization supported by Loyola University Maryland's Office of Student Activities.

Eclectic and provocative, Apprentice House titles intend to entertain as well as spark dialogue on a variety of topics. Financial contributions to sustain the press's work are welcomed. Contributions are tax deductible to the fullest extent allowed by the IRS.

To learn more about Apprentice House books or to obtain submission guidelines, please visit www.ApprenticeHouse.com.

Apprentice House
Communication Department
Loyola University Maryland
4501 N. Charles Street
Baltimore, MD 21210
Ph: 410-617-5265 • Fax: 410-617-2198
info@apprenticehouse.com

Printed in the USA
CPSIA information can be obtained
at www.ICGtesting.com
CBHW051121011124
16771CB00010B/462

9 781627 201438